William Watson

**The Prince's Quest**

And Other Poems

William Watson

**The Prince's Quest**
*And Other Poems*

ISBN/EAN: 9783744711494

Printed in Europe, USA, Canada, Australia, Japan

Cover: Foto ©Thomas Meinert / pixelio.de

More available books at **www.hansebooks.com**

# THE PRINCE'S QUEST

# PUBLISHERS' NOTE

*This very early work of Mr. William Watson's, though little read at the time of its first appearance, thirteen years ago, attracted the attention even then of a few excellent judges, amongst whom Dante Rossetti was, perhaps, the best known. Mr. William Sharp, in his 'Sonnets of the Century,' tells us that Rossetti's copy of 'The Prince's Quest' passed eventually into his hands, with the painter-poet's laudatory marginal annotations. So long ago as 1880, Rossetti, writing to Mr. Hall Caine, spoke of Mr. Watson's 'real and high gifts' (see Caine's 'Recollections of Dante Gabriel Rossetti,' p. 197); and in the same letter Rossetti was at pains to defend Mr. Watson from the charge, preferred against him by some reviewer, of indebtedness to Mr. William Morris. 'He goes right back,' says Rossetti, 'to Keats, with a little modification.' The marked dissimilarity between the manner of 'The Prince's Quest' and its author's later style, will probably constitute a point of somewhat curious interest for readers who care to note the phenomena of a poet's artistic development.*

*The author wishes us to say, that while recognising the crudity and immaturity of many things in this volume, he considers that no alteration less than radical would suffice to remove such defects, and has therefore thought fit to allow these poems—written in great part during his 'teens—to reappear without emendation of any kind.*

*E. M. & J. L.*

1893.

# THE PRINCE'S QUEST

### AND OTHER POEMS BY

## WILLIAM WATSON

## LONDON

ELKIN MATHEWS AND

JOHN LANE

1893

# CONTENTS

|  | PAGE |
|---|---|
| THE PRINCE'S QUEST . . . . . | I |
| ANGELO . . . . . . . | 109 |
| THE QUESTIONER . . . . . . | 124 |
| THE RIVER . . . . . . . | 126 |
| CHANGED VOICES . . . . . . | 128 |
| A SUNSET . . . . . . . | 129 |
| A SONG OF THREE SINGERS . . . . | 131 |
| LOVE'S ASTROLOGY . . . . . | 133 |
| THREE FLOWERS . . . . . . | 134 |
| THREE ETERNITIES . . . . . | 136 |
| LOVE OUTLOVED . . . . . . | 138 |
| VANISHINGS . . . . . . . | 142 |
| BEETHOVEN . . . . . . . | 143 |
| GOD-SEEKING . . . . . . | 144 |
| SKYFARING . . . . . . . | 145 |

# THE PRINCE'S QUEST

## PART THE FIRST

THERE was a time, it passeth me to say
How long ago, but sure 'twas many a day
Before the world had gotten her such store
Of foolish wisdom as she hath,—before
She fell to waxing grey with weight of years
And knowledge, bitter knowledge, bought with
   tears,—
When it did seem as if the feet of time
Moved to the music of a golden rhyme,
And never one false thread might woven be
Athwart that web of worldwide melody.

A

'Twas then there lived a certain queen and king,

Unvext of wars or other evil thing,

Within a spacious palace builded high,

Whence they might see their chiefest city lie

About them, and half hear from their tall towers

Its populous murmur through the daylight hours,

And see beyond its walls the pleasant plain.

One child they had, these blissful royal twain ;

Of whom 'tis told—so more than fair was he—

There lurked at whiles a something shadowy

Deep down within the fairness of his face ;

As 'twere a hint of some not-earthly grace,

Making the royal stripling rather seem

The very dreaming offspring of a dream

Than human child of human ancestry :

And something strange-fantastical was he

I doubt not.   Howsoever he upgrew,

And after certain years to manhood drew

Nigh, so that all about his father's court,

Seeing his graciousness of princely port,

Rejoiced thereat; and many maidens' eyes
Look'd pleased upon his beauty, and the sighs
Of many told I know not what sweet tales.

So, like to some fair ship with sunlit sails,
Glided his youth amid a stormless sea,
Till once by night there came mysteriously
A fateful wind, and o'er an unknown deep
'Bore him perforce.   It chanced that while in sleep
He lay, there came to him a strange dim dream.
'Twas like as he did float adown a stream,
In a lone boat that had nor sail nor oar
Yet seemed as it would glide for evermore,
Deep in the bosom of a sultry land
Fair with all fairness.   Upon either hand
Were hills green-browed and mist-engarlanded,
And all about their feet were woods bespread,
Hoarding the cool and leafy silentness
In many an unsunned hollow and hid recess.
Nought of unbeauteous might be there espied;

But in the heart of the deep woods and wide,
And in the heart of all, was Mystery—
A something more than outer eye might see,
A something more than ever ear might hear.
The very birds that came and sang anear
Did seem to syllable some faery tongue,
And, singing much, to hold yet more unsung.
And heard at whiles, with hollow wandering tone,
Far off, as by some aery huntsmen blown,
Faint-echoing horns, among the mountains wound,
Made all the live air tremulous with sound.

So hour by hour (thus ran the Prince's dream)
Glided the boat along the broadening stream ;
Till, being widowed of the sun her lord,
The purblind day went groping evenward :
Whereafter sleep compelled to his mild yoke
The bubbling clear souls of the feathered folk,
Sealing the vital fountains of their song.
Howbeit the Prince went onward all night long

And never shade of languor came on him,
Nor any weariness his eyes made dim.
And so in season due he heard the breath
Of the brief winds that wake ere darkness' death
Sigh through the woods and all the valley wide :
The rushes by the water answering sighed :
Sighed all the river from its reedy throat.
And like a wingèd creature went the boat,
Over the errant water wandering free,
As some lone seabird over a lone sea.

And Morn pale-haired with watery wide eyes
Look'd up.  And starting with a swift surprise,
Sprang to his feet the Prince, and forward leant,
His gaze on something right before him bent
That like a towered and templed city showed,
Afar off, dim with very light, and glowed
As burnished seas at sundawn when the waves
Make amber lightnings all in dim-roof'd caves
That fling mock-thunder back.  Long leagues away,

Down by the river's green right bank it lay,
Set like a jewel in the golden morn :
But ever as the Prince was onward borne,
Nearer and nearer danced the dizzy fires
Of domes innumerable and sun-tipt spires
And many a sky-acquainted pinnacle,
Splendid beyond what mortal tongue may tell ;
And ere the middle heat of day was spent,
He saw, by nearness thrice-magnificent,
Hardly a furlong's space before him lie
The City, sloping to the stream thereby.

And therewithal the boat of its own will
Close to the shore began to glide, until,
All of a sudden passing nigh to where
The glistering white feet of a marble stair
Ran to the rippled brink, the Prince outsprang
Upon the gleamy steps, and wellnigh sang
For joy, to be once more upon his feet,
Amid the green grass and the flowers sweet.

So on he paced along the river-marge,
And saw full many a fair and stately barge,
Adorned with strange device and imagery,
At anchor in the quiet waters lie.
And presently he came unto a gate
Of massy gold, that shone with splendid state
Of mystic hieroglyphs, and storied frieze
All overwrought with carven phantasies.
And in the shadow of the golden gate,
One in the habit of a porter sate,
And on the Prince with wondering eye looked he,
And greeted him with reverent courtesy,
Saying, ' Fair sir, thou art of mortal race,
The first hath ever journeyed to this place,—
For well I know thou art a stranger here,
As by the garb thou wearest doth appear ;
And if thy raiment do belie thee not,
Thou shouldst be some king's son.  And well I wot,
If that be true was prophesied of yore,
A wondrous fortune is for thee in store ;

For though I be not read in Doomful Writ,
Oft have I heard the wise expounding it,
And, of a truth, the fatal rolls declare          ·
*That the first mortal who shall hither fare*
*Shall surely have our Maiden-Queen to wife,*
*And while the world lives shall they twain have life.'*

.

Hereat, be sure, the wonder-stricken youth,
Holden in doubt if this were lies or truth,
Was tongue-tied with amaze, and sore perplext,
Unknowing what strange thing might chance him next.
And ere he found fit words to make reply,
The porter bade a youth who stood hard by
Conduct the princely stranger, as was meet,
Through the great golden gate into the street,
And thence o'er all the city, wheresoe'er
Was aught to show of wonderful or fair.

With that the Prince, beside his willing guide,
Went straightway through the gate, and stood inside

The wall, that, builded of a rare white stone,

Clasp'd all the city like a silver zone.

And thence down many a shining street they passed,

Each one appearing goodlier than the last,

Cool with the presence of innumerous trees

And fountains playing before palaces.

And whichsoever way the Prince might look,

Another marvel, and another, took

His wildered eyes with very wonderment.

And holding talk together as they went,

The Prince besought his guide to tell him why

Of all the many folk that passed them by

There was not one that had the looks of eld,

Or yet of life's mid-years; for they beheld

Only young men and maidens everywhere,

Nor ever saw they one that was not fair.

Whereat the stripling: 'Master, thou hast seen,

Belike, the river that doth flow between

Flowers and grasses at the city's feet?'

And when the Prince had rendered answer meet,

' Then,' said the other, ' know that whosoe'er
Drinks of the water thou beheldest there
(It matters not how many are his years)
Thenceforward from that moment he appears
Like as he was in youthly days, before
His passèd summers told beyond a score:
And so the people of this land possess
Unto all time their youth and comeliness.'


Scarce had his mouth made answer when there rose
Somewhat of tumult, ruffling the repose
Of the wide splendid street; and lifting up
His eyes, the Prince beheld a glittering troop
Of horsemen, each upon a beauteous steed,
Toward them coming at a gentle speed.
And as the cavalcade came on apace,
A sudden pleasure lit the stripling's face
Who bore him company and was his guide;
And ' Lo, thou shalt behold our queen,' he cried,—
' Even the fairest of the many fair;

With whom was never maiden might compare
For very loveliness!'   While yet he spake,
On all the air a silver sound 'gan break
Of jubilant and many-tongued acclaim,
And in a shining car the bright queen came,
And looking forth upon the multitude
Her eyes beheld the stranger where he stood,
And roundabout him was the loyal stir :
And all his soul went out in love to her.

But even while her gaze met his, behold,
The city and its marvels manifold
Seemed suddenly removed far off, and placed
Somewhere in Twilight ; and withal a waste
Of sudden waters lay like time between ;
And over all that space he heard the queen
Calling unto him from her chariot ;
And then came darkness.   And the Dream was not.

## PART THE SECOND

A FEARFUL and a lovely thing is Sleep,
And mighty store of secrets hath in keep ;
And those there were of old who well could guess
What meant his fearfulness and loveliness,
And all his many shapes of life and death,
And all the secret things he uttereth.
But Wisdom lacketh sons like those that were,
And Sleep hath never an interpreter :
So there be none that know to read aright
The riddles he propoundeth every night.

And verily, of all the wondrous things
By potence wrought of mortal visionings
In that dark house whereof Sleep hath the keys—

Of suchlike miracles and mysteries
Not least, meseems, is this among them all:
That one in dream enamourèd should fall,
And ever afterward, in waking thought,
Worship the phantom which the dream hath brought.
Howbeit such things have been, and in such wise
Did that king's son behold, with mortal eyes,
A more than mortal loveliness, and thus
Was stricken through with love miraculous.

For evermore thereafter he did seem
To see that royal maiden of his dream
Unto her palace riding sovranly;
And much he marvelled where that land might be
That basking lay beneath her beauty's beams,
Well knowing in his heart that suchlike dreams
Come not in idleness but evermore
Are Fate's veiled heralds that do fly before
Their mighty master as he journeyeth,
And sing strange songs of life and love and death.

And so he did scarce aught but dream all day
Of that far land revealed of sleep, that lay
He knew not where; and musing more and more
On her, the mistress of that unknown shore,
There fell a sadness on him, thus to be
Vext with desire of her he might not see
Yet could not choose but long for; till erewhile
Nor man nor woman might behold the smile
Make sudden morning of his countenance,
But likest one he seemed half-sunk in trance,
That wanders groping in a shadowy land,
Hearing strange things that none can understand.
How after many days and nights had passed,
The queen, his mother well-beloved, at last,
Being sad at heart because his heart was sad,
Would e'en be told what hidden cause he had
To be cast down in so mysterious wise:
And he, beholding by her tearful eyes
How of his grief she was compassionate,
No more a secret made thereof, but straight

Discovered to her all about his dream—

The mystic happy marvel of the stream,

A fountain running Youth to all the land;

Flowing with deep dim woods on either hand

Where through the boughs did birds of strange song flit:

And all beside the bloomy banks of it

The city with its towers and domes far-seen.

And then he told her how that city's queen

Did pass before him like a breathing flower,

That he had loved her image from that hour.

'And sure am I,' upspake the Prince at last,

'That somewhere in this world so wide and vast

Lieth the land mine eyes have inly seen;—

Perhaps in very truth my spirit hath been

Translated thither, and in very truth

Hath seen the brightness of that city of youth.

Who knows?—for I have heard a wise man say

How that in sleep the souls of mortals may,

At certain seasons which the stars decree,

From bondage of the body be set free

To visit farthest countries, and be borne
Back to their fleshly houses ere the morn.'

At this the good queen, greatly marvelling,
Made haste to tell the story to the king ;
Who hearing laughed her tale to scorn.   But when
Weeks followed one another, and all men
About his person had begun to say
'What ails our Prince?   He groweth day by day
Less like the Prince we knew . . . wan cheeks, and eyes
Hollow for lack of sleep, and secret sighs . . .
Some hidden grief the youth must surely have,'—
Then like his queen the king himself wox grave ;
And thus it chanced one summer eventide,
They sitting in an arbour side by side,
All unawares the Prince passed by that way,
And as he passed, unmark'd of either—they
Nought heeding but their own discourse—could hear
Amidst thereof his own name uttered clear,
And straight was 'ware it was the queen who spake,

And spake of him; whereat the king 'gan make
Answer in this wise, somewhat angerly :
'The youth is crazed, and but one remedy
Know I, to cure such madness—he shall wed
Some princess; ere another day be sped,
Myself will bid this dreamer go prepare
To take whom I shall choose to wife; some fair
And highborn maiden, worthy to be queen
Hereafter.'—So the Prince, albeit unseen,
Heard, and his soul rebelled against the thing
His sire had willed; and slowly wandering
About the darkling pleasance—all amid
A maze of intertangled walks, or hid
In cedarn glooms, or where mysterious bowers
Were heavy with the breath of drowsèd flowers—
Something, he knew not what, within his heart
Rose like a faint-heard voice and said 'Depart
From hence and follow where thy dream shall lead.'
And fain would he have followed it indeed,
But wist not whither it would have him go.

B

Howbeit, while yet he wandered to and fro,
Among his thoughts a chance remembrance leapt
All sudden—like a seed, that long hath slept
In earth, upspringing as a flower at last,
When he that sowed forgetteth where 'twas cast;
A chance remembrance of the tales men told
Concerning one whose wisdom manifold
Made all the world to wonder and revere—
A mighty mage and learn'd astrologer
Who dwelt in honour at a great king's court
In a far country, whither did resort
Pilgrims innumerable from many lands,
Who crossed the wide seas and the desert sands
To learn of him the occult significance
Of some perplexing omen, or perchance
To hear forewhisperings of their destiny
And know what things in aftertime should be.
' Now surely,' thought the Prince, ' this subtle seer,
To whom the darkest things belike are clear,
Could read the riddle of my dream and tell

Where lieth that strange land delectable
Wherein mine empress hath her dwelling-place.
So might I look at last upon her face,
And make an end of all these weary sighs,
And melt into the shadow of her eyes!'
Thus musing, for a little space he stood
As holden to the spot ; and evil, good,
· Life, death, and earth beneath and heaven above,
Shrank up to less than shadows,—only Love,
With harpings of an hundred harps unseen,
Filled all the emptiness where these had been.

But soon, like one that hath a sudden thought,
He lifted up his eyes, and turning sought
The halls once more where he was bred, and passed
Through court and corridor, and reached at last
His chamber, in a world of glimmer and gloom.
Here while the moonrays filled the wide rich room,
The Prince in haste put off his courtly dress
For raiment of a lesser sumptuousness

(A sober habit such as might disguise
His royal rank in any stranger's eyes)
And taking in his hand three gems that made
Three several splendours in the moonlight, laid
These in his bosom, where no eye might see
The triple radiance; then all noiselessly
Down the wide stair from creaking floor to floor
Passed, and went out from the great palace-door.

Crossing the spacious breadth of garden ground,
Wherein his footfalls were the only sound
Save the wind's wooing of the tremulous trees,
Forth of that region of imperial ease
He fared, amid the doubtful shadows dim,
No eye in all the place beholding him;
No eye, save only of the warders, who
Opened the gates that he might pass therethrough.

And now to the safe-keeping of the night
Intrusted he the knowledge of his flight;

And quitting all the purlieus of the court,

Out from the city by a secret port

Went, and along the moonlit highway sped.

And himself spake unto himself and said

(Heard only of the silence in his heart)

' Tarry thou here no longer, but depart

Unto the land of the Great Mage ; and seek

· The Mage ; and whatsoever he shall speak,

Give ear to that he saith, and reverent heed ;

And wheresoever he may bid thee speed,

Thitherward thou shalt set thy face and go.

For surely one of so great lore must know

Where lies the land thou sawest in thy dream :

Nay, if he know not that,—why, then I deem

The wisdom of exceeding little worth

That reads the heavens but cannot read the earth.'

## PART THE THIRD

So without rest or tarriance all that night,
Until the world was blear with coming light,
Forth fared the princely fugitive, nor stayed
His wearied feet till morn returning made
Some village all a-hum with wakeful stir ;
And from that place the royal wayfarer
Went ever faster on and yet more fast,
Till, ere the noontide sultriness was past,
Upon his ear the burden of the seas
Came dreamlike, heard upon a cool fresh breeze
That tempered gratefully a fervent sky.
And many an hour ere sundown he drew nigh
A fair-built seaport, warder of the land
And watcher of the wave, with odours fanned

Of green fields and of blue from either side ;—
A pleasant place, wherein he might abide,
Unknown of man or woman, till such time
As any ship should sail to that fair clime
Where lived the famous great astrologer.

Entered within its gates, a wanderer
. Besoiled with dust and nowise richly drest,
Yet therewithal a prince and princeliest
Of princes, with the press of motley folk
He mixed unheeded and unknown, nor spoke
To any, no man speaking unto him,
But, being wearied sore in every limb,
Sought out a goodly hostel where he might
Rest him and eat and tarry for the night :
And having eaten he arose and passed
Down to the wharves where many a sail and
    mast
Showed fiery-dark against the setting sun :
There, holding talk with whom he chanced upon,

In that same hour by great good hap he found
The master of a vessel eastward-bound
Upon the morrow for that selfsame port
Whither he sought to go (where dwelt at court
The mage deep-read in starry charact'ry).
An honest man and pleasant-tongued was he,
This worthy master-mariner; and since
He had no scorn of well-got gain, the Prince
Agreed to pay him certain sums in gold,
And go aboard his vessel, ere were told
Two hours of sunlight on the coming day;
And thus agreed they wended each his way,
For the dark hour was nigh, and all the West
Lay emptied of its sun.   But as he pressed
Up the long seaward-sloping street that ran
Through half the town, the Prince sought out a man
Who dealt in pearls and diamonds and all
Manner of stones which men do precious call;
To whom the least of his three gems he sold
For a great price, and laden with the gold

Forthwith returned unto his hostelry
And dreamed all night of seaports and the sea.

Early the morrow-morn, a fair soft gale
Blowing from overland, the ship set sail
At turning of the tide ; and from her deck
The Prince gazed till the town was but a speck,
And all the shore became a memory :
'And still he gazed, though more he might not
    see
Than the wide waters and the great wide sky.
And many a long unchangeful day went by
Ere land was sighted, but at length uprose
A doubtful dusky something, toward the close
Of the last hour before one sultry noon :
Most like an isle of cloud it seemed, but soon
The sailors knew it for the wishèd strand,
And ere the evenfall they reached the land,
And that same night the royal wanderer lay
In a strange city, amid strange folk, till Day

Rose from the dim sea's lap and with his wings
Fanned into wakefulness all breathing things.

Then he uprose, but going forth that morn
A sadness came upon him, and forlorn
He felt within himself, and nowise light
Of heart : for all his lonely travel might
Prove void and fruitless and of no avail
(Thus pondered he), and should it wholly fail,
What then were left him for to do ?   Return
To his own country, that his kin might learn
To know him duped and fooled of fantasies,
Blown hither and thither by an idle breeze
From Dreamland ? Or in lieu, perchance, of this,
Wander unresting, reft of hope and bliss,
A mariner on a sea that hath no coast,
Seeking a shade, himself a shade, and lost
In shadows, as a wave is lost i' the sea.

Thus in a heart not lightsome pondered he,

And roamed from unfamiliar street to street,
Much marvelling that all he chanced to meet
Showed faces troubled as his own : for some
Did weep outright, and over all a gloom
Hung, as a cloud that blotteth out the sun.
Wherefore the Prince addressed him unto one
Of sadder visage even than the rest,
Who, ever as he walked, or beat his breast
Or groaned aloud, or with his fingers rent
His robe, and, being besought to say what meant
This look of rue on all men's faces, cried
In loud amazement, ' What, can any abide
Within this city, having ears to hear,
Yet know not how this morn the mighty seer
Hath died and left the land all desolate ?
For now, when sudden ills befall the state,
There will be none to warn or prophesy
As he, but when calamities are nigh
No man will know till they be come and we
Be all undone together, woe is me ! '

Thus ended he his outcry, and again
Passed on his way and mixed with other men
Scarce joyfuller than he, if less they spake.
Meanwhile upon the Prince's heart there brake
Grief like a bitter wind, beneath whose breath
Hope paled and sickened well-nigh unto death :
For lo, those dumb and formless fears that
  came
Within his heart that morn, and, like a flame
That flickers long and dimly ere it die,
Tarried and would not pass, but fitfully
Flickered and flared and paled and flared again,—
Lo, those mysterious messengers of pain,
Dumb formless fears, were they not verified?
And lo, that voyage o'er the waters wide,
Was it not vain and a most empty thing?
And what might now the years avail to bring,
But hopes that barren live and barren die?

Thus did his heart with many an inward sigh

Ask of itself, though answer there was none
To be returned : and so the day, begun
Tristfully, trailed an ever wearier wing ;
Till toward night another questioning
Like a strange voice from far beset his soul :
And as a low wind wails for very dole
About a tarn whereof the listless wave
· Maketh no answer to its plaining, save
A sound that seems the phantom of its own,
So that low voice making unbidden moan
No answer got, saving the many sighs
Its echoes ; and in this reproachful wise,
Heaping new pain on him disconsolate,
The low voice spake and spake, importunate :
*O Prince that wast and wanderer that art,*
*Say doth love live within thy hidden heart*
*(Love born of dream but nurtured wakingly)*
*Ev'n as that Once when thy soul's eyes did see*
*Love's visible self, and worshipt ? Or hast thou*
*Fall'n from thy faith in Her and Love ere now,*

*And is thy passion as a robe outworn ?*

*Nay, love forbid !   Yet wherefore art thou lorn*

*Of hope and peace if Love be still thine own ?*

*For, were the wondrous vision thou hast known*

*Indeed Love's voice and Fate's (which are the same)*

*Then, even as surely as the vision came,*

*So surely shall it be fulfilled, if faith*

*Abide in thee ; but if thy spirit saith*

*Treason of Love or Fate, and unbelief*

*House in thy heart, then surely shall swift grief*

*Find thee, and hope (that should be as a breath*

*Of song undying) shall even die the death,*

*And thou thyself the death-in-life shalt see,*

*O Prince that wast, O wanderer that shalt be !*


So spake the Voice.   And in the pauses of

That secret Voice there 'gan to wake and move,

Deep in his heart, a thing of blackest ill —

The shapeless shadow men call Doubt, until

That hour all unacquainted with his soul :

And being tormented sore of this new dole,

There came on him a longing to explore
That sleep-discovered flowery land once more,
Isled in the dark of the soul; for he did deem
That were he once again to dream The Dream,
His faith new-stablishèd would stand, and be
No longer vext of this infirmity.
And so that night, ere lying down to sleep,
There came on him, half making him to weep
And half to laugh that such a thing should be,
A mad conceit and antic fantasy
(And yet more sad than merry was the whim)
To crave this boon of Sleep, beseeching him
To send the dream of dreams most coveted.
And ere he lay him down upon his bed,
A soft sweet song was born within his thought;
But if he sang the song, or if 'twas nought
But the soul's longing whispered to the soul,
Himself knew hardly, while the passion stole
From that still depth where passion lieth prone,
And voiced itself in this-like monotone :

'O Sleep, thou hollow sea, thou soundless sea,
Dull-breaking on the shores of haunted lands,
Lo, I am thine : do what thou wilt with me.


But while, as yet unbounden of thy bands,
I hear the breeze from inland chide and chafe
Along the margin of thy muttering sands,


Somewhat I fain would crave, if thou vouchsafe
To hear mine asking, and to heed wilt deign.
Behold, I come to fling me as a waif


Upon thy waters, O thou murmuring main !
So on some wasteful island cast not me,
Where phantom winds to phantom skies complain,


And creeping terrors crawl from out the sea,
(For such thou hast)—but o'er thy waves not cold
Bear me to yonder land once more, where She

Sits throned amidst of magic wealth untold .
Golden her palace, golden all her hair,
Golden her city 'neath a heaven of gold !

So may I see in dreams her tresses fair
Down-falling, as a wave of sunlight rests
On some white cloud, about her shoulders bare,
Nigh to the snowdrifts twain which are her breasts.'

So ran the song,—say rather, so did creep,
With drowsy faltering feet unsure, till Sleep
Himself made end of it, with no rude touch
Sealing the lips that babbled overmuch.
Howbeit the boon of boons most coveted
Withholden was, and in that vision's stead
Another Dream from its dim hold uprose,
Which he who tells the tale shall straight disclose.

C

## PART THE FOURTH

THAT night he dreamed that over him there stole
A change miraculous, whereby his soul
Was parted from his body for a space,
And through a labyrinth of secret ways
Entered the world where dead men's ghosts abide
To seek the Seer who yestermorn had died.
And there in very truth he found the Seer,
Who gazing on him said, 'What wouldst thou here,
O royal-born, who visitest the coasts
Of darkness, and the dwellings of the ghosts?'

Then said the Prince, 'I fain would know to find
The land as yet untrod of mortal-kind
Which I beheld by gracious leave of Sleep.'
To whom the Spirit: 'O Prince, the seas are deep

And very wide betwixt thee and that land,
And who shall say how many days do stand,
As dim-seen armèd hosts between thy bliss
And thee?—Moreover, in the world there is
A certain Emerald Stone which some do call
The Emerald of the Virtues Mystical
(Though what those Virtues Mystical may be
None living knows); and since, O youth, to me
Thou dost apply for counsel, be it known
Except thou have this wondrous emerald stone,
Go seek through all the world, thou shalt not find
The land thou wouldst: but like the houseless
    wind
That roams the world to seek a resting-place,
Thou through inhospitable time and space
Shalt roam, till time and space deliver thee
To spaceless, timeless, mute eternity.

'For in a certain land there once did dwell
(How long ago it needs not I should tell)

At the king's court a great astrologer,
Ev'n such as erst was I, but mightier
And far excelling; and it came to pass
That he fell sick; and very old he was;
And knowing that his end was nigh, he said
To him that sat in sorrow by his bed,
" O master well-beloved and matchless king,
Take thou and keep this lowly offering
In memory of thy servant "; whereupon
The king perceived it was a gem that shone
Like the sea's heart: and on one side of it
This legend in an unknown tongue was writ—
*Who holdeth Me may go where none hath fared*
*Before, and none shall follow afterward.*
So the king took the bright green stone betwixt
His fingers, and upon the legend fixed
His eyes, and said unto the dying Seer,
" Now who shall render this dark scripture clear
That I may know the meaning of the gift ? "
And the mage oped his mouth and strove to lift

His voice, but could not, for the wishèd word
Clave to his rattling throat, that no man heard :
Whereby the soul, departing, bore away
From all men living, even to this day,
The secret. And the jewel hath passed down
Seven times from sire to son, and in the crown
It shineth of that country's kings, being called
Ev'n to this day the mystic emerald ;
But no man liveth in the world, of wit
To read the writing that is on it writ.'

'O Master,' said the Prince, 'and wilt not thou
Instruct me where to find the king who now
Weareth the jewel in his diadem?'
To whom the Spirit, 'O youth, and if the gem
Be worth the finding, is 't not also worth
The little pain of seeking through the earth?—
Yet so thou may'st not wander witlessly,
Look thou forget not this I tell to thee :

When in thy journeyings thou shalt dream once more
The fateful dream thou haddest heretofore,
That filled thy veins with longing as with wine,
Till all thy being brimm'd over—by that sign
Thou mayest know thyself at last to be
Within the borders of his empery
Who hath the mystic emerald stone, whose gleam
Shall light thee to the country of thy dream.'

' But,' said the Prince, ' when all the world's high-
    ways
My feet have trod, till after length of days
I reach the land where lies the wondrous stone,
How shall I make so rare a thing mine own ?
For had I riches more than could be told,
What king would sell his jewels for my gold ?
And on this wise the answer of the Seer
Fell in the hollow of his dreaming ear :
' Behold this Iron Chain,—of power it is
To heal all manner of mortal maladies

In him that wears it round his neck but once,

Between the sun's downgoing and the sun's

Uprising : take it thou, and hold it fast

Until by seeking long thou find at last

The king that hath the mystic emerald stone :

And having found him, thou shalt e'en make known

The virtues lodged within this charmèd chain :

· Which when the king doth hear he will be fain

To have possession of so strange a thing ;

And thou shalt make a bargain with the king

To give the Iron Chain in bartery

For that mysterious jewel whereof he

Knows not the secret worth.   And when at last

The emerald stone in thy own hands thou hast,

Itself shall guide thee whither thou wouldst go—

Ev'n to the land revealed of Sleep, where no

Grief comes to mar their music, neither sound

Of sighing, while the golden years go round.'

So spake the Spirit unto him that dreamed,

And suddenly that world of shadow seemed

More shadowy; and all things began to blend
Together: and the dream was at an end.

Then slept the Prince a deep sweet sleep that knew
Nor dream nor vision; till the dawnlight grew
Up, and his soul a sudden halt did make
About the confines dim of sleep and wake,
Where wandering lights and wildered shadows meet.
But presently uprising to his feet
From tarriance in that frontier-region dim,
Exceeding wonderment laid hold on him;
For even while from off his bed he rose,
He heard a clinking as of metal, close
Thereby, and could in nowise understand;
And lo, the Iron Chain was in his hand!

## PART THE FIFTH

So, being risen, the Prince in brief while went
Forth to the market-place, where babblement
Of them that bought and them that sold was one
Of many sounds in murmurous union —
A buzzing as of bees about their hives,
With shriller gossiping of garrulous wives
Piping a tuneless treble thereunto:
In midst whereof he went his way as who
Looketh about him well before he buys,
To mark the manner of their merchandise;
Till chancing upon one who cried for sale
A horse, and seeing it well-limb'd and hale,
And therewithal right goodly to behold,
He bought the beast and paid the man in gold,

And having gotten him the needful gear
Rode from the market, nothing loth to hear
Its garrulous wives no longer, and the din
Of them that daily bought and sold therein.
So from the place he passed, and slowly down
Street after street betook him till the town
Behind him and the gates before him were,
And all without was cornland greenly fair.

And through the cornland wending many a
    mile,
And through the meadowland, he came erewhile
To where the highways parted, and no man
Was nigh to tell him whitherward they ran ;
But while he halted all in doubtful mood,
An eagle, as if mourning for her brood
Stolen, above him sped with rueful cry ;
And when that he perceived the fowl to fly
Plaining aloud, unto himself he said,
' Now shall yon mournful mother overhead

Instruct the wandering of my feet, and they
Shall follow where she leadeth ': and away
The bird went winging westward clamorously,
That westward even in her wake went he.
And it may be that in his heart there stirred
Some feeling as of fellowship with the bird ;
For he, like her, was bound on a lone quest ;
And for his feet, as for her wings, no rest
Might be, but only urgence of desire,
And one far goal that seemed not ever nigher.

So through that country wended he his way,
Resting anights, till on the seventh day
He passed unwares into another land,
Whose people's speech he could not under-
    stand—
A tract o'errun with tribes barbarian,
And blood-red from the strife of man with man :
And truly 'twas a thing miraculous
That one should traverse all that rude land thus,

And no man rid him of his gold, nor raise
A hand to make abridgment of his days ;
But there was that about him could make men's
Hearts, ere they knew it, yield him reverence,—
Perchance a sovran something in his eye,
Whereat the fierce heart failed, it wist not why ;—
Perchance that Fate which (hovering like a doubt
Athwart his being) hemmed him roundabout,
Gloomed as a visible shadow across his way,
And made men fearful.  Be this as it may,
No harm befell him in that land, and so
He came at last to where the ebb and flow
Of other seas than he had wandered o'er
Upflung to landward an attempered roar ;
And wandering downward to the beach, he clomb
To topmost of a tall gray cliff, wherefrom
He saw a smoke as of men's houses, far
Off, from a jutting point peninsular
Uprising : whence he deemed that there a town
Must surely be.  And so he clambered down

The cliff, and getting him again to horse
Thither along the seabound held his course,
And reached that city about sunset-tide
The smoking of whose hearths he had espied.

There at an hostel rested he, and there
Tarried the coming of the morn. But ere
He fell asleep that night, a wandering thought,
Through darkling byways of the spirit brought,
Knock'd at his soul for entrance, whispering low,
'What if to-night thou dream The Dream, and know
To-morrow, when thou wakest from that bliss,
The land wherein thou liest to be his
Who hath the mystic jewel in his keep?'
So, full of flattering hope he fell asleep,
And sleeping dreamed, but dreamed not that he
    would:
For at one time it seemed as if he stood
Alone upon a sterile neck of land,
Where roundabout him upon either hand

Was darkness, and the cry of a dark sea,
And worldwide vapours glooming thunderously;
And ever as he stood, the unstable ground
Slid from beneath his feet with a great sound,
Till he could find no foothold anywhere
That seemed not unsubstantial as the air.
At otherwhiles he wandered all alone
About a lonely land, and heard a moan
As of some bird that sang and singing grieved;
And peering all about the woods thick-leaved
If so he might espy the bird, he found
At length, after long searching, that the sound
Even from the bottom of his own heart came,
And unawares his own mouth sang the same.
And then in dream 'twas like as years went by,
And still he journeyed, hardly knowing why,
Till at the last a mist about him fell,
And if the mist were death he could not tell,
For after that he knew no more.   And so
He slept until the cock began to crow.

Then came the gladful morn, that sendeth sick
Dreams flying, and all shapes melancholic
That vex the slumbers of the love-distraught.
Unto his heart the merry morning brought
Cheer, and forewhisperings of some far-off rest,
When he should end in sweet that bitter quest.
But going forth that morn, and with his feet
Threading the murmurous maze of street and street,
All strangely fell upon him everywhere
The things he saw and heard of foul or fair.
The thronging of the folk that filled the ways;
The hubbub of the street and market-place;
The sound of heavy wain-wheels on the stones;
The comely faces and ill-favoured ones;
The girls with apple-cheeks and hair of gold;
The grey locks and the wrinkles of the old;—
All these remote and unfamiliar
Seem'd, and himself a something from afar,
Looking at men as shadows on the wall
And even the veriest shadow among them all.

But now when all things dreamwise seemed to swim
About the dubious eyes and ears of him,
That nothing in the world might be believed,
It chanced that on a sudden he perceived
Where one that dealt in jewels sat within
His doorway, hearkening to the outer din,
As who cared nowise to make fast his ears
Against the babble of the street-farers :
Whereat the merchant, seeing a stranger pass,
Guessed by his garb what countryman he was,
And giving him good-day right courteously
Bespake him in his mother-tongue ; for he
Had wandered in his youth o'er distant seas
And knew full many lands and languages.
Wherefore with him the royal stranger fell
To talking cheerly, and besought him tell
Whence all his gems were had and costly things,
Talismans, amulets, and charmèd rings :
Whereto the other answered, They had come
Some from a country not far hence, and some

From out a land a thousand leagues away

To eastward, ev'n the birthplace of the Day,

The region of the sun's nativity ;

And giving ear to this right readily

The Prince would fain be told of him the way

To that far homeland of the youngling Day.

So, being ask'd, the other answered, ' Sir,

· There liveth but one master-mariner

Whose ship hath sailed so far : and that is he

Who hither brought the jewels thou dost see.

And now, as luck will have it for the nonce,

He wills to voyage thitherward but once

Before he dies—for he is old like me—

And even this day se'nnight saileth he.

Wherefore if thou be fain to see that land,

There needeth only gold within thy hand :

For gold, if that it jingle true and clear,

Hath still a merry music for man's ear,

And where is he that hateth sound of it ? '

So saying, the merchant bade the stranger sit,

D

But the Prince thanked him for his courtesy,
And went his way.   And that day se'nnight he
Was sailing toward the far-off morningland,
And felt the skies about him like a band,
And heard the low wind uttering numerous noise,
And all the great sea singing as one voice.

# PART THE SIXTH

EVEN as one voice the great sea sang.  From out
The green heart of the waters roundabout,
Welled as a bubbling fountain silvery
The overflowing song of the great sea ;
Until the Prince, by dint of listening long,
Divined the purport of that mystic song ;
(For so do all things breathe articulate breath
Into his ears who rightly hearkeneth)
And, if indeed he heard that harmony
Aright, in this wise came the song of the sea.

' Behold, all ye that stricken of love do lie,
Wherefore in manacles of a maiden's eye

Lead ye the life of bondmen and of slaves ?
Lo, in the caverns and the depths of Me
A thousand mermaids dwell beneath the waves :
A thousand maidens meet for love have I,
Ev'n I, the virgin-hearted cold chaste sea.

Behold, all ye that weary of life do lie,
There is no rest at all beneath the sky
Save in the nethermost deepness of the deep.
Only the silence and the midst of Me
Can still the sleepless soul that fain would sleep ;
For such, a cool death and a sweet have I,
Ev'n I, the crystal-hearted cool sweet sea.

Behold, all ye that in my lap do lie,
To love is sweet and sweeter still to die,
And woe to him that laugheth me to scorn !
Lo, in a little while the anger of Me
Shall make him mourn the day that he was born :
For in mine hour of wrath no ruth have I,
Ev'n I, the tempest-hearted pitiless sea.'

So sang the waters, if indeed 'twere they
That sang unto the Prince's ears that day,
Since in the ship was not a soul besides
Could hear that burden of the voiceful tides;
For when he told the sailors of this thing,
And ev'n what words the waters seemed to sing,
They stared astonishment, and some, that had
More churlish souls than others, held him mad,
And laughed before his face outright.   But when
The captain heard the gossip of his men
Touching this marvel, the strange news begot
No merry mood in him, who wist not what
Should be the meaning of the miracle,
Nor whether 'twere an omen good or ill.
Wherefore the old seafarer—having heard
The tale retold with many an afterword
The mariner's own most fruitful wit supplied
To grace the telling—took the Prince aside,
And ask'd him sundry questions privily
Concerning this same singing of the sea.

So the Prince told him all there was to tell,
And when that he had heard, the old man fell
To meditating much, and shook his head
As one exceeding ill at ease, and said,
' I doubt the singing thou hast heard was no
Voice of the waters billowing below,
But rather of some evil spirit.near,
Who sought with singing to beguile thine ear,
Spreading a snare to catch the soul of thee
In meshes of entangling melody,
Which taketh captive the weak minds of men.
Therefore if thou shouldst hear the sound again,
Look thou content thee not with hearkening,
But cast thine eyes around, and mark what thing
Thou seëst, and let no man know but me.'

So spake the white-haired wanderer of the
    sea.
And on the morrow—when the sea-line grew
O'erhazed with visible heat, and no wind blew,

And the half-stifled morning dropt aswoon
Into the panting bosom of the noon—
There came unto the Prince's ears anew
The song that yestermorn had hearkened to.
And lifting up his eyes in hope to see
What lips they were that made such melody
. And filled him with the fulness of their sound,
He saw the sun at highest of his round
Show as a shield with one dark bloodstain blurred,
By reason of the body of some great bird
Like to an eagle, with wide wings outspread,
Athwart the sunfire hovering duskly red.
So to the master of the ship he told
What he had witnessed, bidding him behold
The marvel with his own eyes if he would;
Who, though he strained his vision all he could,
Yet might not once endure to look the sun
I' the face; and calling to him one by one
The whole ship's crew, he bade each mariner look
Sunward who could, but no man's eyes might brook

The glare upon them of the noontide rays
And lidless fervour of that golden gaze :
So none of them beheld the bodeful bird.

Then said the greybeard captain, hardly heard
Amid the babble of voices great and small,
' The bird thou seëst is no bird at all,
But some unholy spirit in guise of one ;
And I do fear that we are all undone
If any amongst us hearken to its voice ;—
For of its mouth, I doubt not, was the noise
Thou heardest as of dulcet carolling,
When at thine ear the waters seemed to sing.'

And truly, many a wiser man than he
Herein had farther strayed from verity ;
For that great bird that seemed to fan the sun's
Face with its wings was even the same as once
Flew screaming westward o'er the Prince's head,
Beguiling him to follow where it fled.

And bird it was not, but a spirit of ill,
Man-hating, and of mankind hated still,
And slave to one yet mightier demon-sprite
Whose dwelling is the shadow of the night.

So the days passed, and always on the next
·The bird-sprite like a baleful vision vexed
The happy-hearted sunlight; and each time
Its false sweet song was wedded to the rhyme
And chime of wind and wave—although it dropped
As honey changed to music—the Prince stopped
His ears, and would not hear; and so the Sprite,
Seeing his charmèd songcraft of no might
Him to ensnare who hearkened not at all,
On the tenth day with dreadful noise let fall
A tempest shaken from the wings of him,
Whereat the eyes of heaven wox thundrous-
        dim,
Till the day-darkness blinded them, and fell
Holding the world in night unseasonable.

And from his beakèd mouth the demon blew
A breath as of a hundred winds, and flew
Downward aswoop upon the labouring bark,
And, covered of the blear untimely Dark,
Clutch'd with his gripple claws the Prince his prey,
And backward through the tempest soared away,
Bearing that royal burden; and his eyes
Were wandering wells of lightning to the skies.

Long time the Prince was held in swound, and
    knew
Nor outer world nor inner, as they flew
From darkness unto darkness; till at last—
The fierce flight over, and his body cast
Somewhere alone in a strange place—the life
Stirred in him faintly, as at feeble strife
With covetous Death for ownership of him.
And 'fore his eyes the world began to swim
All vague, and doubtful as a dream that lies
Folded within another, petal-wise.

And therewithal himself but half believed
His own eyes' testimony, and perceived
The things that were about him as who hears
A distant music throbbing towards his ears
At noontide, in a flowery hollow of June,
And listens till he knows not if the tune
And he be one or twain, or near or far,
But only feels that sound and perfume are,
And tremulous light and leafy umbrage: so
The Prince beheld unknowing, nor fain to know.

About him was a ruinous fair place,
Which Time, who still delighteth to abase
The highest, and throw down what men do
    build,
With splendid prideful barrenness had filled,
And dust of immemorial dreams, and breath
Of silence, which is next of kin to death.
A weedy wilderness it seemed, that was
In days forepast a garden, but the grass

Grew now where once the flowers, and hard by
A many-throated fountain had run dry
Which erst all day a web of rainbows wove
Out of the body of the sun its love.
And but a furlong's space beyond, there towered
In middest of that silent realm deflowered
A palace builded of black marble, whence
The shadow of a swart magnificence
Falling, upon the outer space begot
A dream of darkness when the night was not.
Which while the Prince beheld, a wonderment
Laid hold upon him, that he rose and went
Toward the palace-portico apace,
Thinking to read the riddle of the place.
And entering in (for open was the door)
From hall to hall he passed, from floor to floor,
Through all the spacious house, and (saving where
The subtle spider had his darksome lair)
No living creature could he find in it.
Howbeit, that by certain writing that was writ

Upon the wall of one dark room and bare,
He guessed that some great sorcerer had there
Inhabited, a slave to his own lust
Of evil power and knowledge, till the dust
Received his dust, and darkness had his soul ;
But ere death took him he had willed the whole
Of his possessions to a Spirit of Ill,
His sometime mate in commerce damnable,
Making him lord of that high house, wherein
The twain had sealed their covenant of sin.

   With that a horror smote the Prince, and
     fain
Would he have fled that evil spirit's domain
And shook its dust from off his feet that hour.
But from a window of the topmost tower
Viewing the dim-leaved wilderness without,
Full plainly he perceived it hemmed about
With waves, an island of the middle sea,
In watery barriers bound insuperably ;

And human habitation saw he none,
Nor heard one bird a-singing in the sun
To lighten the intolerable stress
Of utter undisputed silentness.

So by these signs he knew himself the thrall
Of that foul spirit unseen, and therewithal
Wholly unfellowed in captivity,
Bound round with fetters of the tyrannous sea.
And sick for very loneliness, he passed
Downward through galleries and chambers vast
To one wide hall wherefrom a vestibule
Opened into a dim green space and cool,
Where great trees grew that various fruitage bore
The like whereof he had not seen before,
And hard by was a well of water sweet;
And being an hungered he did pluck and eat
The strange fair fruit, and being athirst did drink
The water, and lay down beside the brink;
Till sleep, as one that droopeth from the skies,
Dropt down and made a mist about his eyes.

## PART THE SEVENTH

But Sleep, who makes a mist about the sense,
Doth ope the eyelids of the soul, and thence
Lifteth a heavier cloud than that whereby
He veils the vision of the fleshly eye.
And not alone by dreams doth Sleep make known
The sealèd things and covert—not alone
In *visions* of the night do mortals hear
The fatal feet and whispering wings draw near
But dimly and in darkness doth the soul
Drink of the streams of slumber as they roll,
And win fine secrets from their waters deep :
Yea, of a truth, the spirit doth grow in sleep.

Howbeit I know not whether as he slept
A voice from out the depth of dream upleapt

And whispered in his ear ; or whether he
Grew to the knowledge blindly, as a tree
Waxes from bloom to fruitage, knowing not
The manner of its growth : but this I wot,
That rising from that sleep beside the spring
The Prince had knowledge of a certain thing
Whereof he had not wist until that hour—
To wit, that two contending spirits had power
Over *his* spirit, ruling him with sway
Altern ; as 'twere dominion now of Day
And now of Dark ; for one was of the light,
And one was of the blackness of the night.

Now there be certain evil spirits whom
The mother of the darkness in her womb
Conceived ere darkness' self ; and one of these
Did rule that island of the middle seas
Hemmed round with silence and enchantment
    dim.
Nothing in all the world so pleasured him

As filling human hearts with dolorousness
And banning where another sprite did bless ;
But chiefly did his malice take delight
In thwarting lovers' hopes and breathing blight
Into the blossoms newly openèd
Of sweet desire, till all of sweet were fled :
And (for he knew what secret hopes did fill
The minds of men) 'twas even now his will
To step between the Prince and his desire,
Nor suffer him to fare one furlong nigher
Unto that distant-shining golden goal
That beacon'd through the darkness to his soul.

And so the days, the sultry summer days,
Went by, and wimpled over with fine haze
The noiseless nights stole after them, as steals
The moon-made shadow at some traveller's
    heels.
And day by day and night by night the Prince
Dwelt in that island of enchantment, since

E

The hour when Evil Hap, in likeness of
An eagle swooping from the clouds above,
Did bind him body and soul unto that place.
And in due time the summer waxed apace,
And in due time the summer waned : and now
The withered leaf had fallen from the bough,
And now the winter came and now the spring ;
Yea, summer's self was toward on the wing
From wandering overseas : and all this while
The Prince abode in that enchanted isle,
Marvelling much at Fortune and her ways.

And by degrees the slowly-sliding days
Gathered themselves together into years,
And oftentimes his spirit welled in tears
From dawn to darkness and from dark to
    dawn,
By reason of the light of life withdrawn.
And if the night brought sleep, a fitful sleep,
The phantoms of a buried time would creep

Out of their hollow hiding-places vast,

Peopling his Present from the wizard Past.

Sometimes between the whirl of dream and dream,

All in a doubtful middle-world, a gleam

Went shivering past him through the chill gray space,

And lo, he knew it for his mother's face,

And wept; and all the silence where he stood

Wept with him. And at times the dreamer would

Dream himself back beneath his father's roof

At eventide, and there would hold aloof

In silence, clothed upon with shadows dim,

To hear if any spake concerning him;

But the hours came and went and went and came,

And no man's mouth did ever name his name.

And year by year he saw the queen and king

Wax older, and beheld a shadowy thing

Lurking behind them, till it came between

His dreamsight and the semblance of the queen,

From which time forth he saw her not : and when

Another year had been it came again,

And after that he saw his sire the king
No more, by reason of the shadowy thing
Stepping between ; and all the place became
As darkness, and the echo of a name.

.        .        .        .        .        .

What need to loiter o'er the chronicle
Of days that brought no change ?   What boots it
  tell
The tale of hours whereof each moment was
As like its fellow as one blade of grass
Is to another, when the dew doth fall
Without respect of any amongst them all ?
Enow that time in that enchanted air
Nor slept nor tarried more than otherwhere,
And so at last the captive lived to see
The fiftieth year of his captivity.
And on a day within that fiftieth year
He wandered down unto the beach, to hear
The breaking of the breakers on the shore,
As he had heard them ofttimes heretofore

In days when he would sit and watch the sea,
If peradventure there some ship might be.
But now his soul no longer yearned as then
To win her way back to the world of men :
For what could now his freedom profit him ?
The hope that filled youth's beaker to its brim
The tremulous hand of age had long outspilled,
And whence might now the vessel be refilled ?
.Moreover, after length of days and years
The soul had ceased to beat her barriers,
And like a freeborn bird that cagèd sings
Had grown at last forgetful of her wings.

And so he took his way toward the sea —
Not, as in former days, if haply he
Might spy some ship upon the nether blue,
And beckon with his hands unto the crew,
But rather with an easeful heart to hear
What things the waves might whisper to his ear
Of counsel wise and comfortable speech.
But while he walked about the yellow beach,

There came upon his limbs an heaviness,
For languor of the sultry time's excess ;
And so he lay him down under a tree
Hard by a little cove, and there the sea
Sang him to sleep.    And sleeping thus he
    dreamed
A dream of very wonderment : him seemed,
The spirit that half an hundred years before
In likeness of an eagle came and bore
His body to that island on a day,
Came yet again and found him where he lay,
And taking him betwixt his talons flew
O'er seas and far-off countries, till they drew
Nigh to a city that was built between
Four mountains in a pleasant land and green ;
And there upon the highest mountain's top
The bird that was no bird at all let drop
Its burthen, and was seen of him no more.

Thereat he waked, and issuing from the door

Of dream did marvel in his heart; because
He found he had but dreamed the thing that was :
For there, assuredly, was neither sea
Nor Isle Enchanted ; and assuredly
He sat upon the peak of a great hill ;
And far below him, looking strangely still,
Uptowered a city exceeding fair to ken,
And murmurous with multitude of men.

## PART THE EIGHTH

Now as it chanced, the day was almost spent
When down the lonely mountain-side he went,
The whitehaired man, the Prince that was ; and ere
He won the silence of the valley where
The city's many towers uprose, the gate
Was closed against him, for the hour was late.
So even as they that have not wherewithal
To roof them from the rain if it should fall,
Upon the grassy ground this king's son lay
And slept till nigh the coming of the day.

But while as any vagabond he slept
Or outcast from the homes of men, there crept
Unto him lying in such sorry sort
A something fairer than the kingliest court

In all the peopled world had witness of—

Even the shadow of the throne of Love,

That from a height beyond all height did
    creep

Along the pavement of the halls of sleep.

O fair and wonderful ! that shadow was

The golden dream of dreams that came across

His youth, full half an hundred years before,

And sent him wandering through the world. Once
    more

In a lone boat that sails and oars had none,

Midmost a land of summer and the sun

Where nothing was that was not fair to see,

Adown a gliding river glided he,

And saw the city that was built thereby,

And saw the chariot of the queen draw nigh,

And gazed upon her in the goodly street ;

Whereat he waked and rose upon his feet,

Remembering the Vision of the Seer,

And what the spirit spake unto his ear :

'When in thy wanderings thou shalt dream once
    more
The fateful dream thou haddest heretofore,
That filled thy veins with longing as with wine
Till all thy being brimm'd over—by that sign
Thou mayest know thyself at last to be
Within the borders of his empery
Who hath the mystic emerald stone, whose gleam
Shall light thee to the country of thy dream.'


Then rose the heart within his heart and said :
' O bitter scornful Fate, in days long dead
I asked and thou denied'st mine asking : now
The boon can nowise profit me, and thou
Dost mock me with bestowal ! ' Thereupon
He fell to thinking of his youthhood gone,
And wept. For now the goal, the longtime-sought,
Was even at hand, ' But how shall I,' he thought,
' I that am old and sad and hoary-haired,
Enter the place for youth and love prepared ?

For in my veins the wellspring of desire
Hath failed, and in mine heart the golden fire
Burneth no more for ever. I draw near
The night that is about our day, and hear
The sighing of the darkness as I go
Whose ancient secret there is none doth know.'

Ev'n so to his own heart he spake full sad,
And many and bitter were the thoughts he had
'Of days that were and days that were to be.
But now the East was big with dawn, and he
Drew nigh the city gates and entered in,
Ere yet the place remurmured with the din
Of voices and the tread of human feet;
And going up the void and silent street,
All in the chill gleam of the new-lit air,
A Thought found way into his soul, and there
Abode and grew, and in brief while became
Desire, and quickened to a quenchless flame:
And holding converse with himself, he said,
'Though in my heart the heart's desire be dead,

And can no more these time-stilled pulses move;
Though Death were lovelier to these eyes than Love,
Yet would these eyes behold, or ere I pass,
The land that mirror'd lay as in a glass
In the deep wells of dream.    And her that is
The sunlight of that city of all bliss,
Her would I fain see once with waking eyes
Whom sleep hath rendered unto vision twice.
And having seen her beauty I would go
My way, even to the river which doth flow
From daylight unto darkness and the place
Of Silence, where the ghosts are face to face.'


So mused the man, and evermore his thought
Gave him no peace.  Wherefore next morn he
    sought
The palace of the king, but on his way
Tarried till nigh the middle of the day
In talk with certain of the city-folk;
Whereby he learned, if that were true they spoke,

How that the king their lord was nigh distract
With torture of a strange disease that racked
Each day his anguished body more and more,
Setting at naught the leeches and their lore.
Which having heard he went before the king,
Who sat upon his throne, delivering
Judgment, his body pierced the while with pain.
And taking from his neck the charmèd chain
Which he had borne about him ever since
That morn miraculous, the unknown Prince
Upspake and said, ' O king, I hold within
My hand a wonder-working medicine
Of power to make thee whole if thou wilt deign
So to be healèd ' ; and he held the chain
Aloft, and straightway told unto the king
The passing worth and wonder of the thing.

Then he that heard stretched forth a hand that
    shook
With sudden fever of half-hope, and took

The chain, and turned it over in his hand
Until his eyes had left no link unscanned.
And on each separate link was character'd
A language that no living ear had heard,
Occult, of secret import, mystic, strange.
Then said the king, 'What wouldst thou in exchange
For this the magic metal thou dost bring?'
And the Prince answered him and said, 'O king,
Even the emerald stone which some do call
The Emerald of the Virtues Mystical.'
And they who thronged the hall of judgment were
Astonished at the stranger who could dare
Ask such a boon; and some base mouths did curl
With sneers, churl whispering to his fellow-churl,
'Who could have deemed the man so covetous,
So void of shame in his great greed?' For thus
It shall be ever underneath the sun,
Each man believing that high hearts are none
Whose own is as the dust he treads on low.

But the king answered saying, 'Be it so.

To-night this chain of iron shall be worn
About my neck, and on the morrow-morn,
If all the pain have left these limbs of mine,
The guerdon thou demandest shall be thine.
But if this torment still tormenteth me,
Thy head and shoulders shall part company,
And both be cast uncoffin'd to the worms.
Open thy mouth and answer if these terms
Content thee.'   And aloud the Prince replied,
' With these conditions I am satisfied' :
Whereafter, rising from his knees, he went
Out from before the king, and was content.

Next morning, when the king awoke, I wis
No heart was lighter in the land than his ;
For all the grievous burden of his pains
Had fall'n from off his limbs, and in his veins
Upleapt the glad new life, and the sick soul
Seemed like its body all at once made whole.
But hardly was the king uprisen before
There knocked and entered at the chamber-door

His chief physician (a right skilful leech,
But given to hollow trickeries of speech,
And artful ways and wiles), who said, ' O king,
Be not deceived, I pray thee.   One good thing
Comes of another, like from like.   The weed
Beareth not lilies, neither do apes breed
Antelopes.   Thou art healèd of thy pain
Not by the wearing of an iron chain—
An iron chain forsooth ! '—(hereat he laughed
As 'twere a huge rare jest) ' but by the draught
Which I prepared for thee with mine own hands
From certain precious simples grown in lands
It irks me tell how many leagues away :
Which medicine thou tookest yesterday.'

Then said the king, ' O false and jealous man,
Who lovest better thine own praises than
Thy master's welfare !   Little 'tis to such
As   thou   that   I   should   be   made   whole ;   but
    much

That men should go before thee, trumpeting
" Behold the man that cured our lord the king." '
And he was sore displeased and in no mood
To hearken.  But the chief physician stood
Unmoved amid this hail of kingly scorn,
With meek face martyr-like, as who hath borne
Much in the name of Truth, and much can bear.
And from the mouth of him false words and fair
So cunningly flowed that in a little while
The royal frown became a royal smile,
And the king hearkened to the leech and was
Persuaded.  So that morn it came to pass
That when the Prince appeared before the throne
To claim his rightful meed, the emerald stone,
The king denied his title to receive
The jewel, saying, ' Think'st thou I believe
Yon jingling chain hath healed my body ?  Nay ;
For whatsoever such as thou may say
I am not found so easy to beguile :
As for the gem thou wouldest, this good while

F

It hath adorned the crown I wear, nor shall
The stone be parted from the coronal.'

Scarce had the false king spoken when behold
Through the high ceiling's goodly fretted gold
A sudden shaft of lightning downward sped
And smote the golden crown upon his head,
Yea, melted ev'n as wax the golden crown.
And from the molten metal there fell down
A grassgreen Splendour, and the Emerald Stone
Tumbled from step to step before the throne,
And lay all moveless at the Prince's feet!
And the king sat upon his royal seat
A dead king, marble-mute : but no man stirred
Or spake : and only silence might be heard.

Then he before whose feet the gem did lie
Said not a word to any man thereby,
But stooped and lifted it from off the floor,
And passing outward from the open door

Put the mysterious jewel in his breast
And went his way, none daring to molest
The stranger.  For the whisper rose and ran,
'Is not the lightning leaguèd with this man?'

## PART THE NINTH

AND passing through the city he went out
Into the fat fields lying thereabout,
And lo, the spirit of the emerald stone
With secret influence to himself unknown
Guided the wandering of his errant feet,
The servants of the errant soul; and sweet
The meadows were, with babble of birds, and noise
Of brooks, the water's voice and the wind's voice.
Howbeit he gave small heed to any of them ;
And now the subtle spirit of the gem
Led him along a winding way that ran
Beyond the fields to where the woods began
To spread green matwork for the mountains' feet ;
A region where the Silence had her seat

And hearkened to the sounds that only she
Can hear—the fall of dew on herb and tree;
The voice of the growing of the grass; the night
Down-fluttering breathless from the heaven's height;
And autumn whispering unawares at times
Strange secrets and dark sayings, wrapt in rhymes
Wind-won from forest branches. At this place
The old man rested for a little space,
Forgetful that the day was wellnigh flown:
But soon the urgent spirit of the stone
Itself re-entered and possessed anew
His soul; and led thereby, and wandering through
A mile of trackless and untrodden ground,
By favour of the rising moon he found
A rude path, broken here and there by rills
Which crossed it as they hurried from the hills.
And going whitherso the wild path went,
A two hours' journeying brought him, wellnigh spent
With toiling upwards, to a mountain pass,
A bleak lone place where no trees grew nor grass,

But on each hand a peak of rock, high-reared,

Uprose : afar the two like horns appeared

Of some great beast, so tapering-tall they were.

And now with forward gaze the wanderer

Stood where the pass was highest and the track

Went downward both ways ; and behind his back

The full moon shone, and lo, before his face

The bright sea glimmered at the mountain's base.

It seemed, what way soever he might turn,

His fate still led him to that watery bourn.


So journeying down the track which lay before,

He came, an hour past midnight, to the shore,

And, looking backward, far above espied

The two sharp peaks, one peak on either side

Of that lone pass ; verily like a pair

Of monstrous horns, the tips far-seen, up there :

And in the nether space betwixt the two,

A single monstrous eye the moon shone through.

Now all this while the spirit of the stone
Had led him forward, he, the old man lone,
Taking no thought of whither he was bound.
And roaming now along the beach he found
A creek, and in the creek, some little way
From where it joined the sea, a pinnace lay
Moored at the marge; and stepping thereinto,
He sat him down, and from his bosom drew
The mystic gem, and placed it at the prow,
That he might watch its paly splendours, how
They lightened here and there, and flashed aflame,
Mocked at the moon and put the stars to shame.
But hardly was the stone out of his hand,
When the boat wrenched her moorings from the
        land,
And swift as any captive bird set free
Shot o'er the shimmering surface of the sea,
The spirit of the emerald guiding her;
And for a time the old man could not stir
For very greatness of astonishment.

But merrily o'er the moonlit waters went
The pinnace, till the land was out of sight,
Far in the dreaming distance.   All that night,
Faster than ever wind in winter blew,
Faster than quarrel flies the bow, she flew.
A moment was a league in that wild flight
From vast to vast of ocean and the night.
And now the moon her lanthorn had withdrawn :
And now the pale weak heralds of the dawn
Lifted the lids of their blear eyes afar :
The last belated straggler of a star
Went home ; and in her season due the morn
Brake on a cold and silent sea forlorn—
A  strange  mute  sea,  where  never  wave  hath
      stirred,
Nor sound of any wandering wind is heard,
Nor voice of sailors sailing merrily :
A sea untraversed, an enchanted sea
From all the world fate-folden ; hemmed about
Of linkèd Dreams ; encompassed with a Doubt.

But not the less for lack of wind went she,
The flying pinnace, o'er that silent sea,
Till those dull waters of enchantment lay
Behind her many a league.   And now her way
Was toward a shining tract of ocean, where
Low winds with bland breath flattered the mild air,
And low waves did together clasp and close,
And skyward yearning from the sea there rose
And seaward yearning from the sky there fell
'A Spirit of Deep Content Unspeakable :
So midway meeting betwixt sky and sea,
These twain are married for eternity,
And rule the spirits of that Deep, and share
The lordship of the legions of the air.

Here winds but came to rest them from their
    wars
With far seas waged.   Here darkness had her stars
Always, a nightly multitudinous birth.
And entering on this happier zone of earth,

The boat 'gan bate her speed, and by degrees
Tempered her motion to the tranquil seas,
As if she knew the land not far ahead,
The port not far : so forward piloted
By that sweet spirit and strong, she held her way
Unveering.   And a little past midday,
The wanderer lifted up his eyes, and right
Before him saw what seemed a great wall, white
As alabaster, builded o'er the sea,
High as the heaven; but drawing nearer he
Perceived it was a mighty mist that lay
Upon the ocean, stretching far away
Northward and southward, and the sun appeared
Powerless to melt its mass.   And while he neared
This cloudy barrier stretching north and south,
A tale once told him by his mother's mouth,
In childhood, while he sat upon her knee,
Rose to remembrance : *how that on the sea*
*Sat somewhere a Great Mist which no sun's heat*
*Could melt, nor wind make wander from its seat.*

*So great it was, the fastest ship would need*

*Seven days to compass it, with all her speed.*

*And they of deepest lore and wisest wit*

*Deemed that an island in the midst of it*

*Bloomed like a rosebush ring'd with snows, a place*

*Of pleasance, folded in that white embrace*

*And chill. But never yet would pilot steer*

*Into the fog that wrapped it round, for fear*

*Of running blindfold in that sightless mist*

*On sunken reefs whereof no mariner wist :*

*And so from all the world this happy isle*

*Lay hidden.* Thus the queen, long since ; and while

He marvelled if the mist before his ken

Could be the same she told of—even then,

Hardly a furlong 'fore the pinnace' prow

It lay : and now 'twas hard at hand : and now

The boat had swept into the folds of it !

But all that vision of white darkness—lit

By the full splendour of the emerald stone

That from the forepart of the pinnace shone—

Melted around her, as in sunder cleft
By that strong spirit of light ; and there was left
A wandering space, behind her and before,
Of radiance, roofed and walled with mist, the floor
A liquid pavement large.  And so she passed
Through twilight immemorial, and at last
Issued upon the other side, where lay
The land no mortal knew before that day.

There  wilding  orchards  faced  the  beach, and
    bare
All manner of delicious fruits and rare,
Such as in gardens of kings' palaces
Trembles upon the sultry-scented trees,
The soul of many sunbeams at its core.
Well-pleased the wanderer landed on this shore,
Beholding all its pleasantness, how sweet
And soft, to the tired soul, to the tired feet.
And so he sat him down beneath the boughs,
And there a low wind seemed to drone and drowse

Among the leaves as it were gone astray
And like to faint forwearied by the way;
Till the persistence of the sound begat
An heaviness within him as he sat:
So when Sleep chanced to come that way, he
found
A captive not unwilling to be bound,
And on his body those fine fetters put
Wherewith he bindeth mortals hand and foot.

When the tired sleeper oped again his eyes,
'Twas early morn, and he beheld the skies
Glowing from those deep hours of rest and dew
Wherein all creatures do themselves renew.
The laughing leaves blink'd in the sun, throughout
Those dewy realms of orchard thereabout;
But green fields lay beyond, and farther still,
Betwixt them and the sun, a great high hill
Kept these in shadow, and the brighter made
The fruitlands look for all that neighbouring shade.

And he the solitary man uprose,

His face toward the mountain beyond those

Fair fields not yet acquainted with the sun ;

And crossed the fields, and climbed the hill, and won

The top ; and journeying down the eastern side

Entered upon a grassy vale and wide,

Where in the midst a pure stream ran, as yet

A youngling, hardly able to forget

The lofty place of its nativity,

Nor lusting yet for union with the sea.

And through this valley, taking for his guide

The stream, and walking by the waterside,

He wandered on, but had at whiles to ford

The lesser brooks that from the mountain poured

Into this greater ; which by slow degrees

Enlarged with such continual soft increase

Became a river broad and fair, but still

As clear as when it flowed a mountain-rill :

And he the wanderer wandering by that stream

Saw 'twas the river he had known in dream.

So day by day he journeyed ; and it chanced
One day he fared till night was well advanced
Ere lying down to sleep ; and when he waked
Next morn, his bones and all his body ached,
And on his temples lay a weary heat,
And with sore pain he got upon his feet.
Yet when he rose and hard at hand espied
The City sloping to the riverside,
With bright white walls and golden port agleam,
Such as he saw them figured in the dream—
Then the blood leapt as fire along his veins
And the o'erwearied limbs forgat their pains.
But when he strove to make what speed he might
Toward the happy haven full in sight,
The feet that would have hastened thereunto
Could not ; and heavily, as old men do,
He fell to earth, and groaned aloud and said,
' Old man, what wouldst thou, with thy silvered head,
Yonder, where all their tresses be as gold
For ever ?—Thou art suffered to behold

The city of thy search; what wilt thou more?
Tarry thou here upon this river shore;
Thou mightest farther go nor find the grass
Greener whereon to lay thy head, and pass
Into the deep dark populous empty land.'


So spake the man, not able to withstand
This dumb remonstrance of the flesh, now first
Thwarting the soul.   Howbeit a mighty thirst
Consumed him, and he crawled unto the brink
Of the clear stream hard by, that he might
        drink
One draught thereof, and with the water still
His deep desire.   When lo, a miracle!
No sooner had he drunken than his whole
Body was changed and did from crown to soul
The likeness of its youthful self put on,
The Prince of half-an-hundred years agone,
Wearing the very garments that he wore
What time his years were but a single score.

Then he remembered how that in The Dream
One told him of the marvel of that stream,
Whose waters are a well of youth eterne.
And night and day its crystal heart doth yearn
To wed its youthhood with the sea's old age;
And faring on that bridal pilgrimage,
Its waters past the shining city are rolled,
And all the people drink and wax not old.

## PART THE TENTH

THAT night within the City of Youth there stood
Musicians playing to the multitude
On many a gold and silver instrument
Whose differing souls yet chimed in glad consent.
And sooth-tongued singers, throated like the bird
All darkness holds its breath to hear, were heard
Chanting aloud before the comely folk,
Chanting aloud till none for listening spoke,
Chanting aloud that all the city rang;
And whoso will may hear the song they sang :—

I

'O happy hearts, O youths and damsels, pray
What new and wondrous thing hath chanced to-day,

O happy hearts, what wondrous thing and new?

Set the gold sun with kinglier-mightful glance,

Rose the maid-moon with queenlier countenance,

Came the stars forth a merrier madder crew,

Than ever sun or maiden-moon before,

Or jostling stars that shook the darkness' floor

With night-wide tremor 'neath their dizzy dance?


Strong is the Sun, but strong always was he;

The Moon is fair, but ever fair showed she;

The Stars are many, and who hath known them few?

As now they be, so heretofore were they:

What is the wondrous thing hath chanced to-day,

O happy hearts, the wondrous thing and new,

Whereof ye are glad together even more

Than of the sunlight or the moonlight or

The light o' the stars that strow the milky-way.


For all your many maidens have the head

In goodly festal-wise engarlanded,

With flowers at noon the banquet of the bees,
And leaves that in some grove at mid-day grew :
And ever since the falling of the dew
Your streets are full of pomps and pageantries,
Laughter and song, feasting and dancing :—nay,
Surely some wondrous thing hath chanced to-day ;
O happy hearts, what wondrous thing and new ?


II


No, no, ye need not answer any word !
Heard have we all—who lives and hath not heard ?—
What thing the sovran Fates have done to-day ;
Who turn the tides of life which way they please,
And sit themselves aloft, aloof, at ease :
Dwellers in courts of marble silence they.
No need to ask what thing the Fates have done
Between the sunrise and the set of sun,
Mute-moving in their twilight fastnesses !

Changeless, aloft, aloof, mute-moving, dim,
In ancient fastnesses of twilight—him
Have they not sent this day, the long-foretold,
The long-foretold and much-desired, of whom
'Twas whilom written in the rolls of doom
How in a dream he should this land behold,
And hither come from worldwide wandering,
Hither where all the folk should hail him king,
Our king foredestined from his mother's womb?

Long time he tarried, but the time is past,
And he hath come ye waited for, at last:
The long-foretold, the much-desired, hath come.
And ye command your minstrels noise abroad
With lyre and tongue your joyance and his laud,
And, sooth to say, the minstrels are not dumb.
And ever in the pauses of our chant,
So for exceeding perfect joy ye pant,
We hear the beating of your hearts applaud!

### III

And she our Queen—ah, who shall tell what hours
She bode his coming in her palace-towers,
Unmated she in all the land alone?
'Twas yours, O youths and maids, to clasp and kiss;
Desiring and desired ye had your bliss:
The Queen she sat upon her loveless throne.
Sleeping she saw his face, but could not find
Its phantom's phantom when she waked, nor wind
About her finger one gold hair of his.

Often when evening sobered all the air,
No doubt but she would sit and marvel where
He tarried, by the bounds of what strange sea;
And peradventure look at intervals
Forth of the windows of her palace walls,
And watch the gloaming darken fount and tree;
And think on twilight shores, with dreaming caves
Full of the groping of bewildered waves,
Full of the murmur of their hollow halls.

As flowers desire the kisses of the rain,
She his, and many a year desired in vain :
She waits no more who waited long enow.
Nor listeth he to wander any more
Who went as go the winds from sea to shore,
From shore to sea who went as the winds go.
The winds do seek a place of rest ; the flowers
Look for the rain ; but in a while the showers
Come, and the winds lie down, their wanderings o'er.

# ANGELO

ETC.

# ANGELO

SEVEN moons, new moons, had eastward set their horns
Averted from the sun ; seven moons, old moons,
Westward their sun-averted horns had set ;
Since Angelo had brought his young bride home,
Lucia, to queen it in his Tuscan halls.
And much the folk had marvelled on that day
Seeing the bride how young and fair she was,
How all unlike the groom ; for she had known
Twenty and five soft summers woo the world,
He twice as many winters take 't by storm.
And in those half-an-hundred winters,—ay,
And in the summer's blaze, and blush of spring,
And pomp of grave and grandiose autumntides,—

Full many a wind had beat upon his heart,
Of grief and frustrate hope full many a wind,
And rains full many, but no rains could damp
The fuel that was stored within ; which lay
Unlighted, waiting for the tinder-touch,
Until a chance spark fall'n from Lucia's eyes
Kindled the fuel, and the fire was love :
Not such as rises blown upon the wind,
Goaded to flame by gusts of phantasy,
But still, and needing no replenishment,
Unquenchable, that would not be put out.

Albeit the lady Lucia's bosom lacked
The ore had made her heart a richer mine
Than earth's auriferous heart unsunned ; from her
Love went not out, in whom there was no love.
Cold from the first, her breast grew frore, and bit
Her kind lord's bosom with its stinging frost.
Because he loved the fields and forests, made
Few banquetings for highborn winebibbers,

Eschewed the city and led no sumptuous life,

She, courtly, sneered at his uncourtliness,

Deeming his manners of a bygone mode.

And for that he was gentle overmuch,

And overmuch forbearant, she despised,

Mocked, slighted, taunted him, and of her scorn

Made a sharp shaft to wound his life at will.

She filled her cup with hate and bade him drink,

And he returned it brimming o'er with love.


And so seven moons had waxed and waned since
 these

Were wedded.  And it chanced, one morn of Spring

Lucia bespake her spouse in even more

Ungentle wise than was her wont, and he,

For the first time, reproved her;—not as one

That having from another ta'en ill words

Will e'en cry quits and barter words as ill;

But like as a father, whom his child

With insolent lips hath wounded, chides the child

Less than he knows it had been wise to do,
Saying within himself : ' The time will come
When thou wilt think on thy dead father, how
Thou mightst have spoken gentlier unto him
One day, when yet thy father was alive :
So shall thy heart rebuke thy heart enow : '—
Ev'n thus did Angelo reprove his wife.

But though the words from his rough-bearded lips
Were like sweet water from the mouth of some
Rock-fountain hewn with elemental hands,
They fell as water cast i' the fire, to be
Consumed with hissing rage.  Her wrath, let loose,
Blew to and fro, and hither and thither, like
A wind that seems to have forgotten whence
It came, and whither it was bidden blow.
She cursed the kinsfolk who had willed that she
Should wed with him ; and cursed herself that gave
Ear to the utterance of their will ; and cursed
The day on which their will became her deed :

Saying—and this he knew not until now—
'Fool, I should ne'er have wedded thee at all,
No, neither thee nor any like to thee,
Had not my father wellnigh forced me to 't.'
And he that hearkened, the Lord Angelo,
Spake not a word, but bowed his head, and went
Forth of his castle to the forest nigh,
And roamed all day about the forest, filled
With grief, and marvelling at her lack of love.

But that which sorelier bruised his breast than ev'n
Lucia's exceeding lack of love for him,
Was this new knowledge, that in taking her
To wife—in the very act of taking her
To wife—himself had crossed the secret will
Of her whose will in all things it had been
His soul's most perfect bliss to gratify.
Wherefore, to make atonement, in some sort,
For this one wrong he deemed that he had done
The woman—this one crossing of her will—

He knelt him down under the brooding shade
Of a huge oak, and vowed 'fore heaven a vow :
To wit, that Lucia never afterward
Should in his hearing utter forth a wish
For aught of earthly but himself would see
That wish fulfilled, if such fulfilment were
An end that mortal man could compass.    Then
Uprising, he beheld the sinking sun
A vast round eye gaze in upon the wood
Through leafy lattice of its nether boughs :
Whereat he turned him castlewards, and owned
A lighter heart than he had borne that day.

Homeward his face no sooner had he set
Than through the woods came riding unto him
A stranger, of a goodly personage,
Young, and right richly habited, who stayed
His horse, and greeted Angelo, and said :
' I pray you, sir, direct me how to find
An hostel, if there be such hereabouts ;

For I have ridden far, and lost my way
Among these woods, and twilight is at hand.'
Then he that heard replied to him that asked,
Saying : ' The nearest inn is farther hence
Than mine own house ; make therefore mine own
    house
Your inn for this one night, and unto such
Poor entertainment as my house affords
You are most welcome.'  So the stranger thanked
In courtly speeches the Lord Angelo,
Gladly accepting hospitalities            .
That were so gladly proffered ; and the two
Fared on together, host and guest that were
To be, until they reached the castle, where
Angelo dwelt, and where his fathers lived
Before him, lords of land, in olden days.


And entering in, the castle's later lord
Led the young signor to the chamber where
The lady Lucia sat, who rose to give

H

The stranger courteous welcome. (When she chose,
Of looks and lips more gracious none than she.)
But soon as she beheld the young man's face,
A sudden pallor seized her own, and back
She started, wellnigh swooning, but regained
Her wonted self as suddenly, declared
'Twas but a momentary sickness went
Arrow-like through her, sharp, but therewithal
Brief as the breath's one ebb and flow ; and which,
Passing, had left her painless as before.
And truly, from that moment she appeared
More brightly beautiful, if Angelo
Erred not, than she had looked for many a day.

So in brief while the stranger-guest sat down,
With host and hostess, to a table charged
With delicate meats, and fragrant fruits, and wine.
And when the meal was over, and themselves
Were with themselves alone—the serving-men
Having withdrawn—a cheerful converse rose

Concerning divers matters old and new.

And Angelo that evening let his tongue

Range more at freedom than he used ; for though

No man was less to prating given than he,

Yet, when he liked his listener, he could make

His mouth discourse in such a wise that few

Had failed to give delighted audience.

For he had learning, and, besides the lore

Won from his books, a better wisdom owned—

A knowledge of the stuff whence books are made,

‘The human mind and all it feeds upon.

And, in his youth a wanderer, he had roamed

O’er many countries, not as one who sees

With eyes alone, and hearkens but with ears ;

Rather as who would slake the thirst of the soul

By sucking wisdom from the breasts of the world.


Wherefore the hours flew lightly, winged with
    words ;

Till Angelo, from telling of his own

Young days and early fortunes good and ill,

Was with remembrance smitten, as it chanced,

Of some old grief 'twas grief to think upon.

And so he changed his theme o' the sudden, donned

A shadowy mask of laboured pleasantry,

And said : 'My wife, sir, hath a pretty gift

Of singing and of luting : it may be

If you should let your tongue turn mendicant—

Not for itself but for its needy kin,

Your ears—she might be got to give an alms

For those twin brethren.' Whereupon the guest

Unto his hostess turned and smiling said :

'That were indeed a golden alms your voice

Could well afford, and never know itself

The poorer, being a mint of suchlike coin.'

And she made answer archly : 'I have oft

Heard flatterers of a woman's singing say

Her voice was silvery :—to compare 't with gold

Is sure a new conceit. But, sir, you praise

My singing, who have not yet heard me sing.'

And he : ' I take it that a woman's speech
Is to her singing what a bird's low chirp
Is to *its* singing : and if Philomel
Chirp in the hearing of the woodman, he
Knows 'tis the nightingale that chirps, and so
Expects nought meaner than its sovereign song.
Madam, 'tis thus your speaking-voice hath given
Earnest of what your singing-voice will be ;
And therefore I entreat you not to dash
The expectations you have raised so high,
By your refusal.'   And she answered him :
' Nay, if you think to hear a nightingale,
I doubt refusal could not dash them more
Than will compliance.   But in very truth,
The boon you crave so small and worthless is,
'Twere miserly to grudge it.   Where's my lute ? '

So saying, she bethought her suddenly—
Or feigned to have bethought her suddenly—
How she had left the lute that afternoon

Lying upon an arbour-seat, when she
Grew tired of fingering the strings of it—
Down in the garden, where she wont to walk,
Her lute loquacious to the trees' deaf trunks.
And Angelo, right glad to render her
Such little graceful offices of love,
And gladder yet with hope to hear her sing
Who had denied his asking many a time,
Awaited not another word, but rose
And said, ' Myself will bring it,' and before
She could assent or disapprove, was gone.

Scarce had he left the chamber, when behold
His wife uprose, and his young stranger-guest
Uprose, and in a trice they cast their arms
About each other, kissed each other, called
Each other *dear* and *love*, till Lucia said :
' Why cam'st thou not before, my Ugo, whom
I loved, who lovedst me, for many a day,
For many a paradisal day, ere yet

I saw that lean fool with the grizzled beard
Who 's gone a-questing for his true wife's lute?'
And he made answer: 'I had come erenow,
But that my father, dying, left a load
Of cumbrous duties I had needs perform—
Dry, peevish, crabbèd business at the best,
Impertinences indispensable,
Accumulated dulness, if you will,
Such as I would not irk your ears withal:
Howbeit I came at last, and nigh a week
Have tarried in the region hereabouts,
Unknown—and yearning for one glimpse of you,
One word, one kiss from you, if even it were
One only and the last; until, to-day,
Roaming the neighbouring forest, I espied
Your husband, guessed it was your husband, feigned
I was a traveller who had lost myself
Among the woods, received from him—ah, now
You laugh, and truly 'tis a famous jest—
A courteous invitation to his house,

Deemed it were churlish to refuse, and so—
And so am here, your Ugo, with a heart
The loyal subject of your sovereign heart,
As in old days.'    Therewith he sat him down,
And softly drawing her upon his knee
Made him a zone of her lascivious arms.

But thus encinctured hardly had he sat
A moment, when, returning, Angelo
Stood at the threshold of the room, and held
The door half-opened, and so standing saw
The lovers, and they saw not him ; for half
The chamber lay in shadow, by no lamp
Lighted, or window to admit the moon :
And there the entrance was, and Angelo.

And listening to their speech a little space,
The fugitive brief moments were to him
A pyramid of piled eternities.
For while he hearkened, Ugo said : 'My love,

Answer me this one question, which may seem
Idle, yet is not;—how much lov'st thou me?'
And she replied : 'I love thee just as much
As I do hate my husband, and no more.'
Then he : 'But prithee how much hatest thou
Thy husband?' And she answered : 'Ev'n as much
As I love thee. To hate him one whit more
Than that, were past the power of Lucia's hate.'
And Ugo : ' If thou lovest me so much,
Grant me one gift in token of thy love.'
Then she : 'What wouldst thou?' And he answered
        her :
'Even thyself; no poorer gift will I.'
But Lucia said : ' Nay, have I not bestowed
My love, which is my soul, my richer self?
My poorer self, which is my body, how
Can I bestow, when 'tis not in mine own
Possession, being his property, forsooth,
Who holds the ecclesiastic title-deeds? . . .
Yet—but I know not . . . if I grant this boon,

Bethink thee, how wilt carry hence the gift?

Quick. For the time is all too brief to waste.'

And Ugo spake with hurrying tongue : 'Right so

To-morrow, therefore, when the sun hath set,

Quit thou the castle, all alone, and haste

To yonder tarn that lies amid the trees

Haply a furlong westward from your house—

The gloomy lakelet fringed with pines—and there

Upon the hither margin thou shalt find

Me, and two with me, mounted all, and armed,

With a fourth steed to bear thee on his back :

And thou shalt fly with me, my Lucia, till

Thou reach my castle in the mountain'd North,

Whose mistress I will make thee, and mine own.'

Then Lucia said : 'But how if Angelo

Pursue and overtake us?' Whereupon

Ugo replied: 'Pursue he may,—o'ertake

He shall not, save he saddle him the wind.

Besides—to grant the impossible—if he

*Were* to o'ertake us, he could only strive

To win you back with argument; wherein
My servants, at their master's bidding, could
Debate with him on more than equal terms :
Cold steel convinces warmest disputants.
Or, if to see the bosom marital
Impierced, would make your own consorted heart
Bleed sympathetic, some more mild—' But she,
The beauteous Fury, interrupted him
With passionate-pallid lips : 'Reproach me not
Beforehand—even in jest reproach me not—
With imputation of such tenderness
For *him*, and *his* life—when thou knowest how
I hate, hate, hate him,—when thou knowest how
I wish, and wish, and wish that he were dead.'


Then Angelo bethought him of his vow ;
And stepping forward stood before the twain ;
And from his girdle plucked a dagger forth ;
And spake no word, but pierced his own heart through.

# THE QUESTIONER

I ASKED of heaven and earth and sea,
Saying : 'O wondrous trinity,
Deign to make answer unto me,
And tell me truly what ye be.'
And they made answer : 'Verily,
The mask before His face are we,
Because 'tis writ no man can see
His face and live' ;—so spake the three.
Then I : 'O wondrous trinity,
A mask is but a mockery—
Make answer yet again to me
And tell if aught besides are ye.'
And they made answer : 'Verily,

The robe around His form are we,

That sick and sore mortality

May touch its hem and healèd be.'

Then I : 'O wondrous trinity,

Vouchsafe once more to answer me,

And tell me truly, what is He

Whose very mask and raiment ye?'

But they replied : 'Of Time are we,

And of Eternity is He.

Wait thou, and ask Eternity ;

Belike his mouth shall answer thee.

# THE RIVER

## I

As drones a bee with sultry hum
When all the world with heat lies dumb,
Thou dronest through the drowsèd lea,
To lose thyself and find the sea.


As fares a soul that threads the gloom
Toward an unseen goal of doom,
Thou farest forth all witlessly,
To lose thyself and find the sea.

## II

My soul is such a stream as thou,
Lapsing along it heeds not how ;
In one thing only unlike thee,—
Losing itself, it finds no sea.

Albeit I know a day shall come
When its dull waters will be dumb ;
And then this river-soul of Me,
Losing itself, shall find the sea.

## CHANGED VOICES

LAST night the sea-wind was to me
A metaphor of liberty,
   And every wave along the beach
A starlit music seemed to be.

To-day the sea-wind is to me
A fettered soul that would be free,
   And dumbly striving after speech
The tides yearn landward painfully.

To-morrow how shall sound for me
The changing voice of wind and sea?
   What tidings shall be borne of each?
What rumour of what mystery

# A SUNSET

WESTWARD a league the city lay, with one
Cloud's imminent umbrage o'er it: when behold,
  The incendiary sun
Dropped from the womb o' the vapour, rolled
'Mongst huddled towers and temples, 'twixt them set
Infinite ardour of candescent gold,
  Encompassed minaret
  And terrace and marmoreal spire
With conflagration: roofs enfurnaced, yet
Unmolten,—columns and cupolas flanked with fire,
  Yet standing unconsumed
  Of the fierce fervency,—and higher
Than all, their fringes goldenly illumed,
Dishevelled clouds, like massed empurpled smoke

I

From smouldering forges fumed :
Till suddenly the bright spell broke
With the sun sinking through some palace-floor
And vanishing wholly.    Then the city woke,
Her mighty Fire-Dream o'er,
As who from out a sleep is raised
Of terrible loveliness, lasting hardly more
Than one most monumental moment ;  dazed
He looketh, having come
Forth of one world and witless gazed
Into another :  ev'n so looked, for some
Brief while, the city—amazed, immobile, dumb.

# A SONG OF THREE SINGERS

## I

WAVE and wind and willow-tree
Speak a speech that no man knoweth ;
Tree that sigheth, wind that bloweth,
   Wave that floweth to the sea :
   Wave and wind and willow-tree.

Peerless perfect poets ye,
Singing songs all songs excelling,
Fine as crystal music dwelling
   In a welling fountain free :
   Peerless perfect poets three !

II

Wave and wind and willow-tree
Know not aught of poets' rhyming,
Yet they make a silver-chiming
  Sunward-climbing minstrelsy,
  Soother than all songs that be.

Blows the wind it knows not why,
Flows the wave it knows not whither,
And the willow swayeth hither
  Swayeth thither witlessly,
  Nothing knowing save to sigh.

# LOVE'S ASTROLOGY

I KNOW not if they erred
Who thought to see
The tale of all the times to be,
Star-character'd ;
I know not, neither care,
If fools or knaves they were.


But this I know : last night
On me there shone
*Two stars* that made all stars look wan
And shamèd quite,
Wherefrom the soul of me
Divined her destiny.

# THREE FLOWERS

I MADE a little song about the rose
And sang it for the rose to hear,
Nor ever marked until the music's close
A lily that was listening near.

The red red rose flushed redder with delight,
And like a queen her head she raised.
The white white lily blanched a paler white,
For anger that she was not praised.

Turning, I left the rose unto her pride,
The lily to her enviousness,
And soon upon the grassy ground espied
A daisy all companionless.

Doubtless no flattered flower is this, I deemed ;
And not so graciously it grew
As rose or lily : but methought it seemed
More thankful for the sun and dew.


*Dear love, my sweet small flower that grew'st among*
   *The grass, from all the flowers apart,—*
*Forgive me that I gave the rose my song,*
   *Ere thou, the daisy, hadst my heart !*

## THREE ETERNITIES

Lo, thou and I, my love,
And the sad stars above,—
Thou and I, I and thou !
Ah, could we lie as now
Ever and aye, my love,
Hand within hand, my love,
Heart within heart, my dove,
    Through night and day
        For ever !

Lo, thou and I, my love,
Up in the sky above,
Where the sun makes his home
And the gods are, my love,

One day may wander from
Star unto star, my love,—
Soul within soul, my love,
   Yonder afar
     For ever!

Lo, thou and I, my love,
Some time shall lie, my love,
Knowing not night from day,
Knowing not toil from rest,—
Breast unto breast, my love,
Even as now for aye:
Clay within clay, my love,
   Clay within clay
     For ever!

# LOVE OUTLOVED

### I

LOVE cometh and love goeth,
And he is wise who knoweth
Whither and whence love flies :
But wise and yet more wise
Are they that heed not whence he flies or whither
Who hither speeds to-day, to-morrow thither ;
Like to the wind that as it listeth blows,
And man doth hear the sound thereof, but knows
Nor whence it comes nor whither yet it goes.

### II

O sweet my sometime loved and worshipt one,
  A day thou gavest me

That rose full-orbed in starlike happiness
And lit our heaven that other stars had none : —
Sole as that westering sphere companionless
    When twilight is begun
And the dead sun transfigureth the sea :
    A day so bright
Methought the very shadow, from its light
    Thrown, were enough to bless
(Albeit with but a shadow's benison)
The unborn days its dark posterity.
    Methought our love, though dead, should be
    Fair as in life, by memory
Embalmed, a rose with bloom for aye unblown.
But lo, the forest is with faded leaves
And our two hearts with faded loves bestrown,
    And in mine ear the weak wind grieves
    And uttereth moan :
'Shed leaves and fallen, fallen loves and shed,
And those are dead and these are more than
    dead ;

And those have known
The springtime, these the lovetime, overthrown,
With all fair times and pleasureful that be.'
And shall not we, O Time, and shall not we
Thy strong self see
Brought low and vanquishèd
And made to bow the knee
And bow the head
To one that is when thou and thine are fled,
The silent-eyed austere Eternity?

### III

Behold a new song still the lark doth sing
Each morning when he riseth from the grass,
And no man sigheth for the song that was,
The melody that yestermorn did bring.
The rose dies and the lily, and no man mourns
That nevermore the selfsame flower returns:
For well we know a thousand flowers will spring,
A thousand birds make music on the wing.

Ay me I fair things and sweet are birds and flowers,
The scent of lily and rose in gardens still,
The babble of beakèd mouths that speak no ill :
And love is sweeter yet than flower or bird,
Or any odour smelled or ditty heard—
Love is another and a sweeter thing.
But when the music ceaseth in Love's bowers,
Who listeneth well shall hear the silence stirred
With aftermoan of many a fretful string :
For when Love harpeth to the hollow hours,
His gladdest notes make saddest echoing.

# VANISHINGS

As one whose eyes have watched the stricken day
Swoon to its crimson death adown the sea,
Turning his face to eastward suddenly
Sees a lack-lustre world all chill and gray,—
Then, wandering sunless whitherso he may,
Feels the first dubious dumb obscurity,
And vague foregloomings of the Dark to be,
Close like a sadness round his glimmering way ;
So I, from drifting dreambound on and on
About strange isles of utter bliss, in seas
Whose waves are unimagined melodies,
Rose and beheld the dreamless world anew :
Sad were the fields, and dim with splendours gone
The strait sky-glimpses fugitive and few.

# BEETHOVEN

O MASTER, if immortals suffer aught
Of sadness like to ours, and in like sighs
And with like overflow of darkened eyes
Disburden them, I know not; but methought,
What time to-day mine ear the utterance caught
Whereby in manifold melodious wise
Thy heart's unrestful infelicities
Rose like a sea with easeless winds distraught,
That thine seemed angel's grieving, as of one
Strayed somewhere out of heaven, and uttering
Lone moan and alien wail : because he hath
Failed to remember the remounting path,
And singing, weeping, can but weep and sing
Ever, through vasts forgotten of the sun.

# GOD-SEEKING

GOD-SEEKING thou hast journeyed far and nigh.
On dawn-lit mountain-tops thy soul did yearn
To hear His trailing garments wander by ;
And where 'mid thunderous glooms great sunsets burn,
Vainly thou sought'st His shadow on sea and sky ;
Or gazing up, at noontide, couldst discern
Only a neutral heaven's indifferent eye
And countenance austerely taciturn.

Yet whom thou soughtest I have found at last ;
Neither where tempest dims the world below,
Nor where the westering daylight reels aghast
In conflagrations of red overthrow :
But where this virgin brooklet silvers past,
And yellowing either bank the king-cups blow.

# SKYFARING

DRIFTING through vacant spaces vast of sleep,
One overtook me like a flying star
And whirled me onward in his glistering car.
From shade to shade the wingèd steeds did leap,
And clomb the midnight like a mountain-steep ;
Till that vague world where men and women are,
Ev'n as a rushlight down the gulfs afar,
Paled and went out, upswallowed of the deep.

Then I to that ethereal charioteer :
'O whither through the vastness are we bound ?
O bear me back to yonder blinded sphere ! '
Therewith I heard the ends of night resound ;
And, wakened by ten thousand echoes, found
That far-off planet lying all too near.

K